STUDY IN PAVILIONS AND SAFE ROOMS

for Chris Warrington

STUDY IN PAVILIONS AND SAFE ROOMS

PAUL FOSTER JOHNSON

PORTABLE PRESS AT YO-YO LABS
NEW YORK

Study in Pavilions and Safe Rooms © Paul Foster Johnson
All rights reserved. 2011

ISBN: 978-0-615-43357-8

Original cover art by Chris Warrington
Design & typesetting by HR Hegnauer

PORTABLE PRESS AT YO-YO LABS
Brooklyn, New York
www.yoyolabs.com

CONTENTS

[I did something emblematic of a Life in the Aughts] 1
Fountain of Friendship 2
Gaylord Texan Panic Room 3
Bowery Safe Room 5
Digital Cities 7
This Tortured Earth 8
Abrasive Machining 10
The Spiral Theater 11
[I did something to prove the desert is not silent] 12
Electrification 13
Portable Survival System 14
The House of Good Taste 15
Folk Education 16
Enya's Panic Room 17
Visual Agitation 18
Amsterdam 19
Sermons from Science 21
Monument to the Plough 22
The Azux 23
Colonnade of States 24
Palace of Youth 25
[I did something at work] 26
Storm Safe Room 27
Lapidary 28
Extreme Water 29
[I did something on an observation deck] 30
Manege 31
Chat Room 32

Physical Plant 34
Kunstkamera 36
Bronx Safe Room 37
Man the Producer 38
[I did something I could never discuss] 39
Skywalk 41
Gaylord Opryland Panic Room 42
Underground World Home 44
Reversible Destiny Panic Room 45
Menagerie 47
Colonial Space Phenomenon Exhibit 48
Urban Beings 53
Palace of Arts 54
Intimate Immensity Safe Room 55
Atomic Raw Material 57
Study in Pavilions 58
[I did something in an enclosed study room] 62

I did something emblematic of a Life in the Aughts
several of us narrated, twitching to repeat a song
encapsulating one feeling. In a hunched posture,
clicking furiously, I was shocked by the self-idealizations
of my enemies. Knowing their limitations I noted well
the eloquent strands of one dressed like a box jellyfish.
An outfit defined the contretemps and form
drew it out forever. Pathos in the guise
of a repeating song buffeted indifferent objects.
No one made tea or borrowed from my life
of beauty. In this life I dedicated myself to deciding
whether I was offended. Here I reenacted something
trying not to look bored because I was not bored
but deeply interested in preserving a record
of all transactions if only to fling it into the ether.

FOUNTAIN OF FRIENDSHIP

Let the ban on graven images exempt the squid flotation
so inelegant on land, for our memory of sisterly affection
in the waves was wiped by bullhorn. This is the danger
of going in for multitudes. You would have to be
plucked out if pushed in by smoldering teens who blurt
their untranslatable deathwish. The message they bear
is think like them lest they win. It departs on its side
leaking adjustments of the new year and the redolence
of vinyl and tape. I turn red emoting (the squid among
my greatest influences) having known the crowd from when
I was left out in the elements to correct my wheezing.
Though the lawn is dead in winter there is major preening
in the trees. Competing with the theme we show
our care for the environment or at any rate disintegrate.

GAYLORD TEXAN PANIC ROOM

for Filip Marinovich

I like how a shadow gets artificially long
if I trust that it veils the unsayable
a convergence that recurs in listening to
songs about drugs when exercising
thinly veiled, sweatsuit inspired
by Oskar Schlemmer
Leigh Bowery and Teletubbies.

The cottonball shrubs are rendered to scale
but you cannot run to the lake as it appears
during undocumented drinking
where divine rays of light over a water attraction
distribute ridiculous comfort.

He emerges out of nowhere
as if from behind chaises longues
experiencing syncope
that gives meaning to procedures
while reading manuals in hill country.

A thorax bearing scars of childhood surgery
condenses every straight boy
who has made himself available.

Here I signal ambivalence about sausagefests
like polluted sunsets or their artificial beauty
always worried that the outcome will be confused
with funk art.

BOWERY SAFE ROOM

Winter clothes retarded them as they went
to sweat the technique of the bad poem

but once there they listened as they stared at the floor
toward which chunks of ceiling gravitated.

They were guyed in community
for what turned out to be a seminar.

The disembodied voice was a friend
and cold ornament released its payload

to the player piano version of "The Entertainer."
Is it because everything is apparent

that they felt haunted?
Is it the specter of offensiveness

behind sense and nonsense?
Though someone was paid to tell them

they were not crafting the well-wrought urn
they didn't know they were being groomed for oblivion.

No text in the body
but hands in formalin.

Research went into the bad poem
and undulating, divine rays

were its lifeblood. Research formed an aspic
a suburban riot that would disperse

if they called an agency to smash it.
They knew nothing when they started

but learned to walk in the truck spew
toward the only thing of significance

accompanied by something of the abyss
in the melancholic tones of people's phones.

DIGITAL CITIES

If a change in relations
is signaled I am oblivious
and gradually depleting
my go-bag.

Let the go-bag be a false index
of preparedness.

Let the go-bag indicate
a pseudoproblem.

Let me find instead abandoned
backpacks in cocktail lounges,
churches,
factories.

It rivets alienation
to look out from one.

THIS TORTURED EARTH

A song for the power station
commences in shadows
ventriloquism of complex contradictions

pyramid of complex contradictions
beautiful cone under an arch.

In a work song for smelting
the occult looms
full of machinery we battle.

      *

The ideal backdrop reproduces frantically
a rampart before disordered sentiment.

The ideal backdrop
is an impediment of leisure
an algorithm that guesses sympathies
before which go our obsessions
with aerated chocolate

clods or throwing stars of our sympathies
falling under freedom of information.

*

Aggressive flowers are painted
over a plastic backdrop coming into its own
over bricks, Kevlar, chicken wire, sympathies
without concordance.

ABRASIVE MACHINING

aided your thought process
you self-styled outsiders
sharpening sticks against your enemies.
Some of us were driven into your arms.
Off-kilter and feline, you worked
under difficult conditions
putting out stapled affairs
that spread delight until forgotten.
Insofar as calling on the forces
of the universe to cancel elections
did not not not prevent a restaging
of the Eighteenth Brumaire
as late as January 2005 we were right.
You could only maneuver around it raggedly.

THE SPIRAL THEATER

Soldiers of an unreported conflict
seize a pavilion

and enforce distance
as they allow the decor

to wash over them.
The energy of the maker, long dead,

is distributed through the hall.
They are sheathed

in effort. The will
held mute in branches.

Glass helmets.
Sapped geist.

I did something to prove the desert is not silent
riding a pony over the dunes.
The pony looked about to die
before it ran. When some good animals die
the taxidermist gives them fangs
and conversely a person can behave
in a satanic fashion but redeem himself
through holistic workshops
in that desert. The people
who teach there are the best.
Afterward you will spread your wings
like a cormorant. When you reenter society
people will invoke Wallace Stevens to make you
feel better about your job and you will.

ELECTRIFICATION

Our communion threw pink light
spottily, without occult resonance.
Mirrors were glued to my face
the picture of lovesickness
the only time I saw camouflage trucks
in Chelsea. Not not not a horizon
hope was a stage of unfreedom
and I regretted casting a lot with irony.
Poiesis can be restrained by a lip ring
and you will have to deal with the aftermath
when foreigners borrow August Kleinzahler
with their library cards.
It is always and never too late
I gushed in vain as the light went out.
Infelicities kept scraping by.

PORTABLE SURVIVAL SYSTEM

The fleck on my tongue is a datum
in the lament of superficiality
in the paean to exclusivity.

I rear my head prehistorically
and filiate with the high-minded.

My job is to love recombinatory potential
though it leads not to radical awareness.

Each pushes against each
seeing something tentacular in the other
something formed in virile maturity.

Traipsing must come to pass
before there can be clarity
but I injured myself
went flying and ate it.

To slip on a carpet of dead periodical cicadas
is very PFJ.

THE HOUSE OF GOOD TASTE

could be a landing site
nonidentical to an illegal venue
shut down after a travesty.
When the sun has its way
it's a dolmen that does not not
not need need need an equal.
It knows that there are banalities
to embrace, that there are popular
and ephemeral phenomena
to embrace. When you are raw,
trapped, or in need of a safehouse
you cannot force its equivalence
with a landing site or distinguish
it from garbage, so you splay
the straw of your drink and breathe
on its lawn and rattle the fence
behind its *hell vermilion curtain.*

FOLK EDUCATION

Their singer suffered breakdowns. In their work
there was a sense of what it was to live there at that time.
One song described the dark around the military
vehicles between them and the cocaine waiting
in Gramercy. It was about the sepsis that followed love
or love repeated as farce, the neck neck neck
damaged by an anonymous hand unstringing guitars.
They got away with it and worked to abolish youth
by knitting and paying half-attention. I thought I was
in love because my sentiments were matched
by a generic, abiding sense of unfreedom. Nothing
survives lovers descrying the red flags of old flames.
Nothing is more relatable than an unreasonable person
operating subtractively, indulgently, out of exasperation.

ENYA'S PANIC ROOM

is reinforced with 500 overlaid vocal tracks
and paintings of the moon.

Paintings that were in your face, thund'rous
pentecostal paintings
virtual not illusory
islands of the ideal backdrop
are uplifting.

This is the direction I am headed
like I'm in a cloud chamber
meandering with some stray things flaring.

It is a sophisticated enclosure
I hope never to use.

Binder clips affixed for draping
turn pain into art
perfecting a cape with sleeves
zhuzhing the Dorian brooding
on the happiest day of my life.

VISUAL AGITATION

I compensate for passions that never claimed to be new
waiting for distortion with a crocodile bag jabbed
at my rib. What I have against it crumbles
and gapes. Lines culminating in exotic skins
leave me suddenly lusting for a tan in something like
a solar puberty, gaily pulling streamers so I can present
something hopeful. Sad I do not not not know
the angels of the facility or the order of their passions
transplanted into sheetrock across the diagonal
from the cafeteria to the elevator. It's the new year
and they are willowy. My loyalty is easy so I clear
the entrance to make of this less a shithole and more
the magic union of subject and object, ungovernable
passions not not not scantly springing into action.

AMSTERDAM

The butoh of our greeting
exposed us as frauds

Coming out of an attic
believing *that people are really good at heart*
as frauds freaking out in a smartshop

We filed into an aquarium
saw something like a koosh
with an eyeball on a stalk
and a translucent seahorse

Navigated away from a pained and ecstatic object

Our revelations unspooled
through an alternate concealed exit
becoming motes in the sunset
not but for to play

An aerosol haze replaced the light
needed to sort through observations
accreted in a small room

But we were not not not defensive about
being sedimented content

Removed from sensate experience
hat decomposing on a parkside path
polyurethane jeans and plaid
crashed into us in the frantic dusk

Until we landed in a sports bar
where there was to be a travesty
a gesture that eventuated a fumble

SERMONS FROM SCIENCE

I look up from your book and try to feed
the catbird red hot nuts. It calls alarms
and sounds into the brush. When I say
your voice comes through there, I do not not not
mean you are finding your voice. I can imagine
your actual voice expressing itself that way.
Marveling at tufted animals will take us as far
as a positive science when we really should bathe
in negativity and the light of retrospect. Maybe
in the elaborate privacy of these works a driver
and a hitchhiker intend to murder one another.
And here you say that someone somewhere
has just now shut herself in to freak out for weeks
and this does not not not only occur in literature.

MONUMENT TO THE PLOUGH

My head and life lines are invisible
but the plough fills in the blanks.
The plough is a frantic reproduction
in aluminum and I am a clown
tipping it toward oblivion.

In a program of self-study the brain
may suggest a formula for industrial weirdness.
In the tourism of crap jobs a brain
abets bad planning, the hand
grasps a glossy red handle, the brain
an isolated piece at draughts.

My job is to remind everyone
that spontaneous order is not natural
and to bus figures to their habituation.
In transit they stretch under layers
that deform their silhouettes
and smoke.

Undispersed among other gamepieces
the brain in a program of self-study
looks into a series of situations in space
amoral virtual homogeneous
much like garbage dumps.

THE AZUX

In my adult life I have found it hard
to lurch from point A to point B
stuck staring at birds circling a stillborn highrise
trapped between the functional
and mystical planes of abstraction
clod in the realm of clods

Coworkers who provoke not through words
but festivals of dread
have made it impossible to live up to dad's
sí se puede

Coworkers themselves have tried to achieve
a taut surface of John Henry
but they knotted themselves up

In the middle of demonic dictation
I have lurched before innumerable openings
pancaking and beginning to flail

COLONNADE OF STATES

Happiness, long in coming, mists the windows
of the theme restaurant. A guard with a cleft
forehead works wordlessly on our compulsion
to submit. Ours is a nation run by military
bureaucracy, but here its absence is generalized
into an atmosphere of control and more
basement bars accommodating travesty.
It becomes necessary to shrug off the Libra need
need need to decode the shiny ties at businesslunch.
Beneath a ring of golden women assembled
from compossible worlds or hallucinations or lies,
I feed the creative principle copious saliva, a sequence
of code spitvalved into headphones that furnish me
with nation language as late as 2006 and hope.

PALACE OF YOUTH

I was enthralled to
a cadre of guys for
whom Beckett was
an ideal father up
in their voids. My
favorite said she was
a lone wolf. I
saw her examine
the ground outside
the library
then break into
a run. She could
not not not stop
adjusting herself
when chucked into
the force field.

I did something at work
flouted a guideline
giving gifts that made contact
with my colleagues' bodies.
So many shared so few
pieces of leather furniture
on a break from abolishing despair
with some contortion.
Mysterious fumes
caused me to smush
consonants together
like in hymns. I saw what was
at first my date with dentistry.
My lazy eye darkened everything
into bullet points bluish
and speaking from a place of hunger.

STORM SAFE ROOM

If you get burned resisting a closed system
you may be paranoid about clarity.

Dust eddies up the street
in sympathy with your nervous illness.

The wind roils a patch of pachysandra
and flowers with petals like dark leaves.

Your disillusionment is a dreamy species
of jellyfish. There are others

who prefer compact propulsive effort.
You are all having simultaneous breaksthrough.

LAPIDARY

When spirituality has recourse to cartoons
Christ appears in German underwear
or dishdasha. Since turning to shamanic practice
for empowerment, I bear down on your book
of daily negations when I am among the headless,
surrounded by khaki. Shifting, I try
to nail nail nail the right carriage
for *the new maladies of the soul*. She says
they must be broken in as she inducts me
into the chamber of wonders. Oh the room
is immaculate. She said it would be
a horn of plenty and it's more like the obelisk
of everything existing. When I need need need more I
just point to what I want with this goatlike extremity.

EXTREME WATER

Maybe the Appassionata will drown out every other
sound in the mall. So happy to be here thanks
to the mastery of a river with concrete, though
my consumer role obliges me to walk away in disgust
and to return with a new offer. The absent copula
makes me unsure. I just shower in palatalized consonants
that fly from gilded mouths. The river must have been
diverted for paving, choked by lily pads and without
an easement for frogs. You would have to be plucked out
if pushed in by the smoldering teens. Their artlessness
and inward turn have the effect of a bluff, so continue,
shoppers, sampling the roe of various nations
without worry. Why come to the mall if not not
not to find an actually existing corner to be insipid in?

I did something on an observation deck
at the bird sanctuary, probably bawled
into wiglike clumps of grass, as C. cast a cold eye
on swan distribution, which changed as they moved
like cardboard cutouts against a screen.

C. looked like he was formulating a thought
but was just trying to remember
painting a painting of this
just what I felt, isolated in squares of sunlight.
The memory of the deck spilled onto a patio.

Now I am waiting for C. to sit in the park
at night and watch the rats joust. I want him
to paint a painting, reform
versus revolution, to add a heart or a sun
and take it out. And then to discard the skeleton.

MANEGE

The one with purple streaks
instigates something
with truckers on the service road.

The message they bear is
think like them
lest they win.

It is the new year
and we are willowy.
The service road is long

on omens.
The more obscure
the more we gape.

CHAT ROOM

P. entered a third space
from which he could watch time pass
instead of walking to the monastery
in the middle of the night.

His opaque sexuality derived from the absence
of a guarantee that his person would remain intact.

He recognized this in himself
and we stared at the pylons regressing
into the lackluster northeastern woods.

The monastery was a display
before which he claimed sangfroid
a picturesque ruin to which he was conveyed
as though by boreal fluid.

Everyone loved occasional works like this
their allusions to complementary and absent events.

Weaving around proliferating drywall
I despaired over this desire.

P. joined the migrant workforce
and grew more disconsolate and distant
and drunk in our presence.

Our presence was only possible
because of advances in technology
in a dialectical relationship with their debasement:
servers in cold rooms
and a recursive void of woodblock chat sounds.

PHYSICAL PLANT

Talk radio intimates my liquidation
over intermittent blasts of steam.

Because already underway
it can be apprehended.

Tears that are a function of cold air
derange my supervisor.

He imagines talk giving way to klaxons
whereupon we'd throw ourselves into a fosse.

Evangelists, we hear you and know
you are all thinking long and hard

about our cupcake atavism.
To appease you we affix naked dolls

to a black cage and wait inside.
Clinging to the cage we want to kiss

the evangelists, the real curators
despite our spiel. We are whisked

along a transverse by a pickup
in constant flight through winter wind.

We trick ourselves into subscribing
to the perspective of a fetus

whose stance was fierce.
Callers are angry

about passing out of objecthood
and into being conduits of sensation

collections of cells cathected
by the immorality of debt.

Callers are angry
about being asked to read into a lacuna.

Often we are required to return to a cage
in the lackluster northeastern woods

with the consolation that the dead
are spared some agency

sometimes winning things
and maintaining semblances worth seeking.

KUNSTKAMERA

It's OK that you look
like one of Peter the Great's
monsters. I like a goblin king
in criminally tight pants.
A level of maturity would be needed
to know what you go through
to be brisk for others. My lack
of understanding hinted at an urtext
looming behind the force
bending away from me.
If it is still there I would line it
with offerings though carrying
loose fruit for this purpose
seems overly suggestive.

BRONX SAFE ROOM

Poverty obliges
a Bronx full of battlements.

Either the crystal city dispersed
or stayed fierce and polygonal
but probably dispersed
into apocalyptic slums.

Racing to the city
lent illusory plenitude
excitement with no object.

When I engaged my mother in my diagnosis
her words radiated mystery.

It's synaesthesia
or a memoir eroded by stress
into so many pixels

or crosscurrents of desire
in the Harlem River
stoked at a distance.

MAN THE PRODUCER

What you make is staked
on the continuation of your life.

What is to be done?

Drag each other around amidships,
asking questions.

*

In its small wooden coffin
a turn of phrase

grows brittle and collapses
as I try to close the loop.

*

Would you rather tame the wild
or let it toss you around?

Flaming out inside a tent
my surprise and admiration
have one tongue.

I did something I could never discuss
made an acquaintance
and embraced him in a phone booth.

While interested parties lurked
among free newspaper boxes
he removed his domino.

What to construe
from leather bracelets?
The impossibility of translation
from a phone booth to a churchyard

a gate painted white
a belfry with no bell
some culture with haceks
the sense of lolling in a park

from a churchyard to a community garden
heckling the rooster as it crowed.

We left the part we liked
jeering the rooster from a sward.

We reentered the garden with a script
but refused to expand on the vestiges of happiness.

A girl took responsibility for the garden
and plied us with background information
until her nervous guardian sent us back to the church
with a coat of arms where we were going anyway
as though under the influence of boreal fluid.

The songbirds of the yard
were about to be contaminated
by a new age concert.

With so little at stake
they praised positive thinking.

SKYWALK

Mount Parnassus is a joke because the gradient
is so slight, a semicircle of saplings and no
alpine concession stand. Resting in the weeds
near the neighboring pavilion's statues
and a 50-foot-tall farm girl, I crave honey
from the best region for honey. I crave meat
even though it is the terror of domestic life.
I can relate to carnivores, having dyed
my hair the universal auburn and thrust
the preponderance of flowers face-down.
To trail behind the busted transport is no choice
bearing flowers for thrift, now paying
for what was gotten by truck, the career of cars
from a pedestrian bridge always a dirge and oddly trellised.

GAYLORD OPRYLAND PANIC ROOM

What is important is not winning, but taking part,
by turns moving them to love us
and putting them to sleep.

Past a cemetery containing hustlers
southerners walk miles, staving off
a travesty of familiar quotations.

After milky shots the evening turns
to vast concrete expanses.
A drunkard reading minds

I give their hospitality its due
as I sit tweaking on a ledge.
The horror-porn mashup of the cemetery

invades a giant hotel
which slides into parody
as southerners steal into it.

They conspire to lure a person to a person
when I only wanted to reenact the bordello flashback
at the end of *Sentimental Education*.

Both approaches form a basis for action
beyond the premise of prowling
past nature dismembering itself.

UNDERGROUND WORLD HOME

The treatment milieu is lush

soft earth strewn
with crutches left as testimonials.

A lack of commitment
has kept me from following suit.

I move through the narrowest
of openings and plunder

a bicycle. I come as a stranger
over a wall and find myself

among the setpieces of a travesty.
Behind the scenes

I shimmy
toward a ruthless criticism of everything existing

uproarious but no longer available.

REVERSIBLE DESTINY PANIC ROOM

for Stacy Szymaszek

We hold strong convictions
and collage them with homosexual graffiti
at comfort stations.
All examples are proprietary.

To cope with information scarcity
we visit an island
as husband and wife and also siblings
interlocking for warmth.

We funnel the good through the bad
suck out the sound
because it is important to do things
that are already done in our name.

You put your whole self in
telegraphing perversion at work.
They who deprive us of sleep
embargo rooms

until *room*
becomes a noumenal
interior of van
upholstered to anticipate clawing.

Cooing at the mention
of a proper name
telegraphs an aroused state activating
pleasant vacant dogma.

In a drearily appointed living room
the shells and nests
of a future containing the past
await perforation.

MENAGERIE

Birds call like lasers
sainted creatures whose flesh's funereal aura
fills the decorated shed.

A more extreme version
of passing out of objecthood
moves us to applaud.

We blend our voices to make overtones
and the dogs bark by instinct
or mechanization or both.

Whether it's thirty chickens rushing out
or one rat murdering another
an animal's worldview is of consequence.

Someone says it's all very lord of the flies
but it's more like direct action in a mall.
It's like winged ants flying into our eyes.

COLONIAL SPACE PHENOMENON EXHIBIT

Under the pretext of education in the use of form
we enter a spatial projection of a four-hex mainframe
to decide whether we flatter ourselves as pioneers.

An exhibit exceeds the travesty
of feeble excursions,
first feeble probes.

Space disappointment
pervades the narrative of progress
and the perfection of travel
deforms each hex
into highly irregular space.

Stars lie incomprehensibly distant
like we never left
the absolute inertial frame.

We transcribe their perturbations
which mirror our dislikes
and conclude that what humanity wants most
is to be left in pods and spires
to birth a civilization
that will not acknowledge
unrepresentable massive traps
of light and sound.

If one cuts a path through hyperspace
in a torch-driven starship of modular design
one develops a simplified relation
to both acceleration
and the first derivative of acceleration
known as *jerk*
at the instant of departure.

We who dislike
laws and political structure
and relish the design of a new world
where there are no misreadings
love jerk.

As a sort of relief valve
when each hex is cathected.

But this simplified relation
does nothing for our desiring
new propulsion sources to break us
of our specialized ways, for instance
the anxiety of finding a job
through a wormhole.

An interest in free and unrestricted development
makes us feel weird about leisure cities.

Our rictus says it all.

In a hunched posture
we overshoot the interactive features
and draw lewd things on the questionnaire.

Two ants on separate paths over a cloth
discover fresh new worlds and then ignore them
discover fresh new worlds and then ignore them
as we might gaze past a planet and into its sun.

Government is in our way
and we want it out
of the airless void of interplanetary space
better to pursue privacy, companionship,
recreation, and exercise
that mark time in warp maneuvers that take forever.

We shall work wherever people need us
in jobs that may not exist on Earth.

The starship captain demystifies space
as a virtual force responding to the power
of the photon drives
the ducts and air movers
summarizing conquest
as the prophylaxis of space
cordoning the limits of knowledge.

We are concerned about our safety on a new planet
but long for an uncomplicated life
just a brain and a nerve center in a residential spire
lit by lomic crystal in a meditation room
maintaining pod access from the mainframe
to the force field wand
through which our likes and dislikes well and disperse.

We long for a feeling of connection to worlds
with a certain tone coursing through
an absolute frame of reference
like in a hollow, a ravine
poring over the work of friends.

We could bring our friends no further
than a picnic, seductive irritation
on the rocks, a withering away
of chalk and limestone, shutting our eyes against
what we did not know had to be recaptured.

The success of this mission
will determine the future of the colonies
their personal robots, food autoselectors,
somafields, and our continued ability
to go round and round in the night
screaming our heads off in alleys
carpeted bars and supermarkets.

Ordinary maser waves
are projected at errant memory
plagued by singularities
by infinity or *infinitesimalness*
that never occurs in nature.

Errant memory rattles
the railings of a sunken family room
in a residential spire full of crystal imagery
that cannot be had on Earth at any price.

No one has an excuse to be bored
with floorshows and optical art.

A prophylaxis of space
only ever extends
the worlds one dances in and out of.

URBAN BEINGS

Without responsibilities you are left
to repent at leisure.

Concrete pulled away reveals the scandal
of trees' gelatinous selves. Selves
I have been chained to.

Birds tear into sacks of prepared foods.
If their aggression were not improvised
they would continue attacking the myrtle.

Saved in an apartment
burnt and looted and/or
unitary and urbane
then layings on of hands
sensitivities and self-parody
concrete floor and insulation
of private meaning.

Our bodies are prisons.
Our prisons are overcrowded metaphors.

PALACE OF ARTS

In condemning Mount Parnassus as a joke
I am bad, dissolute, literally dissolved, unwilling
to be seduced by curatorial prowess, by rows
of bushes appearing as ground-glass opacities
in the lungs of the dead space. My bad unblocked
approach overruns it. I thought it was impenetrable
and should have known it was not not not from what
it exuded. I.e., the surrounding sky aflame with truth
receding to invisibility. Once in the booth I look out
through a one-way glass. The space was killed
by the lack of spontaneity of you-know-who.
His hidebound vision could not not not foresee
our being thwacked by hanging wires, our being
scarred for life in disassembled exhibition halls.

INTIMATE IMMENSITY SAFE ROOM

The germ of the house
is a paraphrase
of the windowless, doorless chamber
we mince toward.

We want to go somewhere even more remote
and see a bald eagle
erasing its kino-pravda
see the fossil record of absence and dread of the inevitable
in a forest setting
after which we can sport fictions.

We want to go to the sea
at low tide, when it gives up prefabricated shelves
and a creature will launch itself upward
suffocating for our benefit.

But I am at work and I mince toward a chamber
my voice is a doorchime
always when my mind goes blank
in the middle of explaining phenomena
in this case *Can we all get along?* taped there to the wall
in paraphrase, its border an abundance
of gingerbread men.

I would not flinch though sensible to typography
insofar as it is conveys a person, like GOD in all caps
or one presently lisping, awakened by art
which it uses to jog something in itself.

It hammers its terms into a shape
as someone branches out from a peach sweater
to a pink shirt, hearing crashing noises
as everything outside backs up.

ATOMIC RAW MATERIAL

Let me be less attracted to anarchy in the new year.
Let me find an outlet for fatal obsessions. Let me grind
on domesticity. I am run down by sepsis from ignoring
the prohibition on the subbasement mattress.
For these bad parts so full of humanity I bow to you.
The shards you inspired sink to the bottom.
Thanks for *the aggression of nationalist traditions*.
Thanks for a first wave of aggression followed by
pictures of dead birds and a disc covered in icing
and spit. You keep probing my willingness to engage
with one block left and longer with the gait
disturbance. Refinement without end has exhausted
me during coffee hour as the fear of making sense
has impressed itself in the dark of all description.

STUDY IN PAVILIONS

for Jessica Mahomond

The river hurls itself into the sea
with acid, bitchery, and clumsiness
as happens when we are asked
to invent improbable scenarios of travel
accounts surcharged by lovesickness
that finally come to be told in English
on a dilating screen
in modular units exclusive of breath.

In a Bay Ridge travel narrative
she curls a horn of hair
into submission, hair and eyes
like team colors in an exhortation
to cultivate personal style
while I confront bisexuality
by rubbing a jewel case demonstratively
over emotion poured onto a bed.

Someday language will ordain
isolated dance moves on a pier and our experience
of wonder will be organized by carousels.

Wonder is a reflex
that allows me to avoid relating
generationally like with a 90s frisson
of NWO or a suspicion that seeming
randomness is purposive.

For days I meant to establish myself
in a carrel, to camp permanently.

What is your relationship to carrels?

Are they where you arrive, snack-laden,
at universals?

It is said that they are underoccupied
before we go there with our sorrows.

Hallucinations projected onto them
would describe an ideal.

Instead an extension of myself
proceeds into the wilderness
between sand-colored buildings.

Fueled by organ music
I wind myself around my inheritance
of monism.

I would rather make my own ether
than have to explain again
that I don't work with images.

My ancestors wrote poems on napkins.

The weeds of the railbed
make me want to prove I am not
the fruit of my father's
modest civilizing mission, desiring
a cigarette in greenery
and it is suspiciously green
with plant fluff in the gutter.

When inventing scenarios of travel
tell a story of infelicitous recurrence
deficient in affect
thriving on awkwardness
not mechanistic
even admitting to being lazy
in love, lazy in research
indulging emotional substitutes
for serious matters as they cluster
around an epiphany or whatall.

If it bear resemblance
to a succession of drones
or the mysterious black boxes
replacing trashcans on subway platforms
secret it into a bower or bus shelter
paranoid spaces, lucky charms
that I hold harmless
best visited after hundreds and hundreds
of thousands of hours of practice.

I did something in an enclosed study room
with film-reading capacity
as the reality of appearance
bound slowness and style.

The appearance of reality
horribly but necessarily flowered
even where there was no sun
to savage books with no horizon
nor nor nor light bouncing.

Thus spoke some experimental people
of revolutions and bodily weakness
sad girls who teased out one idea for ten years.

No rest for the weary
scratched into the surrounding wood.

The names of the girls were not revealed
because they resembled the living and the dead.

As they spoke, their smoking habit
suggested access to the underworld.

Their voices carried something leathery from beyond,
a quality so good and steeped in sadness.

Most of us represented a demimonde
taking a beating in a state of emergency.

Most of us were working on our
Chinese Democracy.

Logical intuitive introverts, we were foxes
among lions, they said, who might still blunder
upon captions to our downfall.

ACKNOWLEDGMENTS

Earlier drafts of poems in this collection appeared in *Jacket* ("A Tonalist" poetry feature, ed. Laura Moriarty), *The Awl* ("Poetry Section," ed. Mark Bibbins), *Cannot Exist* (ed. Andy Gricevich), and *GAM* (ed. Stacy Szymaszek).

"Colonial Space Phenomenon Exhibit" was written for a reading to benefit the Reanimation Library in Brooklyn, New York, on December 1, 2009. The poem includes language from *Handbook of Space Pioneers: Guide for Pioneers from Earth to the Eight Planets Now Available for Colonization* by L. Stephen Wolfe and Roy L. Wysack (1979).

Thanks to Julian T. Brolaski, E. Tracy Grinnell, Kathleen Miller, Akilah Oliver, and Tim Peterson, who provided helpful comments early on. The "I did something..." poems are dedicated to Rachel Levitsky. I am especially grateful to Brenda Iijima for her enthusiasm and encouragement, and to the Council of Literary Magazines and Presses and the Jerome Foundation for their support through the FACE OUT program.

FACE OUT
maximizing the **VISIBILITY** of emerging **WRITERS**